Pressing RESET for Kids

Ⓞriginal strength

Copyright © 2020 OS Press.

ALL RIGHTS RESERVED. This book contains material protected under International and Federal Copyright Laws and Treaties. Any unauthorized reprint or use of this material is prohibited. No part of this book may be reproduced or transmitted in any form or by any means, electronic or mechanical, including photocopying, recording, or by any information storage and retrieval system without express written permission from the author/publisher.

Contributors:
Suzie Gullet - bentonfitness.com
Michelle Nicholson Photography - Michellenicholsonphotography.com
Dani Almeyda - originalstrengthinstitute.com
Tim Anderson - originalstrength.net

ISBN: 978-1-64184-220-4

Be a SuperMover

Your body is awesomely and wonderfully made. You were designed to feel super hero strong, for your whole life.

Even now, as a kid, you are so much stronger than you think!

You might fall down, and get hurt, but you were designed to heal. This means that no matter how old (or young) you are, or what you like to do, or how you like to play, you have a super power already inside of you. This super power is that you have a strong body with healing powers.

Pretty cool, right?

Your body really is awesome. So awesome that it can move and bend and push and pull in all sorts of crazy ways. You can run, dance, crawl, skip, climb, wrestle, throw, jump, and hug.

Our bodies love to move, matter of fact, that's what our bodies were made.... to move!

Moving the way we were designed to move makes us strong in both the inside and the outside. Moving helps our muscles, and it is very important for keeping our brain strong and healthy too.

The more we move, the stronger we get and the smarter we get!

Your brain is also strong, and it not only controls what you think but also how you move and how you feel. Sometimes we have played a lot, or we are doing a lot of school work, or maybe we are sad, or maybe we are frustrated or mad.

Sometimes, we just need to RESET ourselves, so we can move better and feel better.

Did you know you can RESET your body and your brain? You sure can!

The way we RESET our body and brain is by moving.

Moving in special ways RESETs your body like pushing the power button on a computer or video game player.

Pressing
RESET

Remember moving the way you were designed allows you to move better, and feel better every day.

Moving is your power button or your superpower.

Think of yourself as a super mover, like a superhero with a power button on your chest.

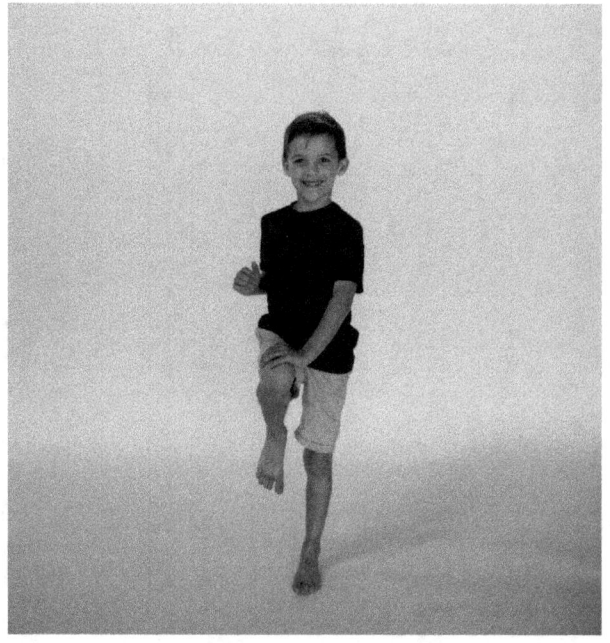

When you Press RESET you will

- Breathe better
- Think better
- Be balanced
- Increase your strength

Resetting your Breath

Rest your head on your desk. Let your tongue come to the roof of your mouth and close your mouth and breathe in and out through your nose.

Imagine your belly is like a balloon. Try to fill up your balloon with air and then slowly let the air out. Then refill the balloon again. Try this for a least one whole minute. It will make you a super mover!

You can practice this anytime and anywhere, by the way. This is a secret to being strong and healthy.

Resetting your breath will also help you think more clearly and make your body ready for stronger movements like running, jumping and climbing.

Resetting your Balance

Did you know you can reset your balance just by moving your head? Yep! Just like when someone asks you a question that you say "YES" to, by nodding your head, or if someone asks you a question that you say "NO" to, by turning your head.

Both of these movements help your body and your mind work better so you can balance better.

Let's try it. Sitting tall in your chair, look up and down like you are nodding "yes." Look down with your eyes as you lower your head and look up to the sky with your eyes as you raise your head. Now turn your head left and right like you're saying "no" or like you are an Owl, trying to look all the way behind you. Look left with your eyes as you turn your head to the left and look right with your eyes as you turn your head to the right.

Can you nod your head up and down for a minute? Can you look left and right for another minute?

Resetting your Strength

When you were younger, you moved around by rolling and crawling everywhere. Now that you are older you move around on two feet by walking, running and skipping. Your body was meant for all of these movements, and they are the ones that make you very strong.

In fact, every time you move on two feet by walking or marching or skipping or running you are helping your body to become stronger.

Let's practice getting stronger with another movement on two feet, **Cross-Marching!**

To begin, stand up nice and tall.

Touch your right hand to your left knee and touch your left hand to your right knee. Do this again and again. It's kind of like marching while touching your opposite arms and legs together. So let's call it Cross-Marching!

Can you do this for a whole minute? Every time you take a step and touch your opposite hand to your opposite knee your body gets a little bit stronger. This also helps your brain get a little smarter too!

These are just 3 ways to RESET your body and help you become a super mover and a super thinker. Let's learn some more!

Pressing RESET

RESET #1

Breathing

Why?

- You were born a "belly breather."
- Your diaphragm (your breathing muscle) helps to protect your spine.
  - » Belly breathing allows you to move well.
- Breathing is the "key" for controlling your emotions.
  - » Belly breathing calms your nervous system, soothes your emotions and allows you to think better.
  - » Breathing up in the neck and chest excites your nervous system, increases your stress, and makes it harder to make good decisions.

Position #1

BELLY BREATHING ON BACK

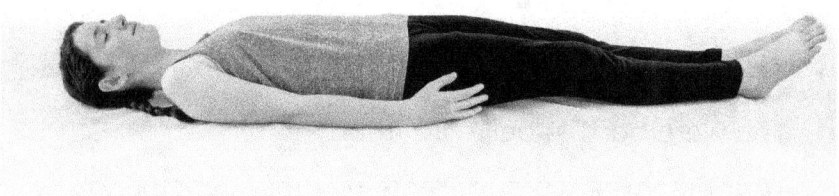

- Lie on your back
- Place the tongue on the roof of your mouth and close your lips
- Take deep breaths in and out of your nose
- Try to fill your belly up with air as if it were a balloon.

Position #2

CROCODILE BREATHING

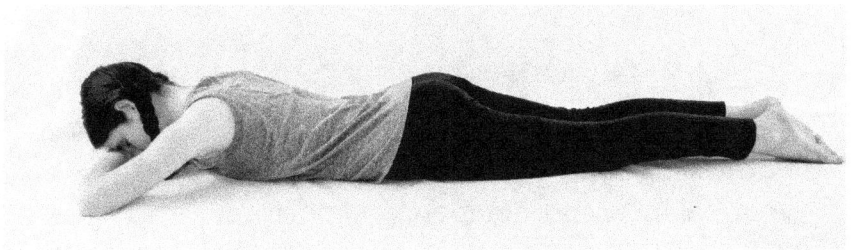

- Lie on your tummy
- Place your tongue on the roof of your mouth and close your mouth
- Take deep breaths in and out of your nose
- Try to fill your belly up with air. Can you feel it push against the floor?

RESET #2
Head Control

Why?

- Controlling the movements of your head improves your balance, coordination, and posture.
- Every muscle in your body is connected to the movements of your head.
  - » The better you can control your head, the better you can control your entire body.
- Head Control is <u>essential</u> to obtaining health and strength throughout your lifetime.

Movement #1

HEAD NODS

- Sit back on your heels like a puppy
- Place your tongue on the roof of your mouth and close your mouth
- Slowly look up to the sky and down to your belly like you are saying YES
- Use your eyes to look up and down
- Remember to breathe like you are filling up a balloon

Movement #2

HEAD TURNS

- Sit back on your heels like a puppy
- Place your tongue on the roof of your mouth and close your mouth
- Turn your head to the right and then left like you are saying NO
- Use your eyes to look left and right as you turn your head
- Keep filling your balloon with air!

RESET #3
Rolling

Why?

- Rolling further improves and strengthens your balance.
- Rolling connects your shoulders to your hips, it connects your torso, making you stronger.
- Rolling is good for the spine.
- Rolling allows you to move with fluid strength and power - rolling makes you strong!

Movement #1

EGG ROLLING

- Lie on your back
- Hold your knees to your chest like a ball
- Place your tongue on the roof of your mouth and close your mouth
- Look with your eyes, then roll your head the way you want to roll and then let your body roll in that same direction → Roll your eyes, then head, then body
- Pretend you are egg rolling from side to side

RESET #4
Rocking

Why?

- Rocking further nourishes the brain and calms the emotions.
- Rocking teaches all your moving parts (your joints) how to play together and become one whole body.
- Rocking teaches the rhythm between the shoulders and the hips, preparing them for crawling and walking.

- Get on your hands and knees like a puppy
- Place your tongue on the roof of your mouth
- Hold your head up
- Rock back and forth, almost like a frog just about to jump

RESET #5
Crawling

Why?

- Crawling connects both halves of the brain together, making it stronger and smarter.
- Crawling reflexively connects the entire body and ties it together.
  » It strengthens the nervous system.
  » It makes the body stronger and faster so that it can move efficiently, gracefully and powerfully.
- Crawling makes you a Super Mover!
  »

- Get on your hands and knees
- Hold your tongue on the roof of the mouth with your lips closed
- Keep your head up
- Crawl forward slowly
    » Your left arm should move with your right leg and your right arm should move with your left leg

Your
DESIGN

The Power in Your Design

The power of movement, the hope of health, healing and the expression of strength all live inside of the nervous system.

Our very design contains the movement program intended to keep us strong, able and healthy. Spending just a few minutes every day relearning or remembering how to do these movements will enable you to live your life better, with strength and health.

Your body truly is awesomely and wonderfully made. It is designed to be strong and able, always. Everything you need to experience this is inside your nervous system waiting for you to move with it. In other words, your Original Strength is inside. It's your move...

Here is a fun routine to RESET your strength and practice becoming a SuperMover. These can be done in a classroom or even at home:

The GetUp Game

- Lie on the floor with your knees in chest
- Roll over like an egg to one side and get up off of the floor until you are standing tall
- Then see if you can get back on the floor the same way you got up.
- Repeat as many times as you can for 3 minutes

Make a Crawling Square

- Get on your hands and knees
- Crawl forward 4 steps
- Crawl sideways to the right 4 steps
- Crawl backward 4 steps
- Crawl sideways to the left 4 steps
- Repeat as many squares as you can for 2 minutes

Make a Cross-Marching Square

- Stand tall
- Cross-march forward 4 steps
- Cross-march sideways to the right 4 steps
- Cross-march backward 4 steps
- Cross-march sideways to the left 4 steps
- Repeat as many squares as you can in 1 minute

The 3-minute Classroom Reset

Try the following 3-minute reset to improve the concentration and atmosphere of the classroom!

1. **Breathe with your diaphragm x 1 minute.**
   Stand up nice and tall. Place your tongue on the roof of your mouth and breathe deep down into your belly.
2. **Rock back and forth x 1 minute.**
   Place something soft on the floor for your knees. Get on your hands and knees, hold your head up and your chest "proud", keep your tongue on the roof of your mouth, continue to breathe down into your belly, and rock back and forth.
3. **Standing coss-march x 1 minute.**
   Stand nice and tall. Touch your opposite limbs together, moving back and forth from side to side. Touch how you can; elbows to knees, forearms to thighs or hands to hips.

Wherever you can reach comfortably, touch your opposite arm to your opposite leg repeatedly for one minute.

Do this and resume a less stressful, calm yet energized class that is ready for learning!

Want to learn more?

This information was designed to give a brief view into the Original Strength System and how to teach your child how to Press RESET.

We put it together because we know Pressing RESET can help everyone and anyone. If your child,does nothing more than what is in this booklet, you will notice many changes in how your child moves and acts. It will benefit both their mind and body...and your's too!

We hope you will encourage your child to Press RESET at home or in school, and that you will consider joining in on these movements with them.

Original Strength is a human movement education company with a mission to make the world a better place through movement.

We do this by conducting workshops, training and certifying coaches and instructors, developing educational materials for PE Teachers, Physical Therapy students, and professionals as well as many other professions dealing with fitness, health, and wellness, sports conditioning, vestibular and neuromuscular functionality.

If you want to know more about Pressing RESET and regaining your original strength, visit www.originalstrength.net. There you will find a variety of books, free video tutorials (Movement Snax), a complete listing of our workshops and OS Certified Professionals near you.

You may want to consider finding an OS Certified Professional. These professionals can conduct an Original Strength Screen and Assessment (OSSA) which is the quickest and easiest way to identify areas your movement system needs to go from good to best. The OSSA allows the Pro to pinpoint the best place for you and your kids to start Pressing RESET and restoring their original strength.

Press RESET now and live life better because you were awesomely and wonderfully made to accomplish amazing things.

For more information:

Original Strength Systems, LLC
101 South Main Street
Suite 221
Fuquay-Varina, NC 27526

919.299.1774

"... I am fearfully and wonderfully made..."
Psalm 139:14

www.ingramcontent.com/pod-product-compliance
Lightning Source LLC
Chambersburg PA
CBHW070120110526
44587CB00016BA/2739